LORD,
I
KEEP
RUNNING
BACK
TO
YOU

Lord, I Keep Running Back to You

Ruth Harms Calkin

Tyndale House
Publishers, Inc.
Wheaton, Illinois

Library of Congress
Catalog Card Number 78-58748
ISBN 0-8423-3820-9
paper
Copyright © 1979
by Ruth Harms Calkin.

Third printing, September 1979.
Printed in the United States
of America.

To You, dear Lord
whose arms are always wide open
when I come running!

CONTENTS

NO ONE,
LORD,
BUT YOU

I KEEP RUNNING BACK TO YOU

You know how it is with me, Lord:
So often I mess up my days.
I judge harshly
I am critical and obstinate
I waste time and energy
I blame others for my failure.
There are people I try to avoid
And tasks I try to evade
And when I can't have my own way
I sulk in my own little corner.
Lord, I even turn my back on You
To escape Your penetrating gaze.

Then finally I get fed up with myself.
The intolerable loneliness frightens me
And I can no longer endure my shame.
It always happens, Lord—
I keep running back to You!

Where else can I go?
Who else understands me so well
Or forgives me so totally?
Who else can save me from foolish pride?
No one, Lord, but You.
So thank You for accepting me
For loving me
For always welcoming me.
I just can't help it, Lord
I keep running back to You!

BEGINNING

Lord
I'm at the end
Of all my resources.

Child
You're just at the beginning
Of Mine.

QUIT

Lord, I've hidden in dark corners
I've wept over my sin
I've confessed it a thousand times
I've tortured myself remembering.
Lord, how sorry do I have to be?

Dear stubborn child
Sorry enough to quit the sin.

TRAGEDY

O God
How heartbreaking
How tragic
That anyone should crawl
From death to death

From darkness to darkness
From fear to fear
When Your lavish offer is
Life! Light! Love!

NOTHING CAN SEPARATE ME

God, who or what in all the world
Can convince me that You
No longer love me—
That You've given me the slip
And thrown me over?
Shall mounting pressures interfere
With my personal relationship with You?
Shall shadowy fears that plague my nights?
Shall a palpitating heart
Or a strange buzzing in my head
Or pounding pain
Or bitter tears?

Or what if people laugh at me and reject me
Until I feel utterly confused and alone?
Or what if I can no longer work
And unpaid bills pour over me
Like a deluge of crashing bricks?
Or what if an accident incapacitates me
And I must depend upon others for personal care?
Or what if I can no longer remember names
And my blurry eyes see double
And my hands tremble?

Or what if an earthquake crumbles my home
And my furniture is buried in thick mud?
Or what if I am left alone
Without family or friends?
Am I finished then?
Does this end my small scene?

No, dear God.
Positively not!
In all these impossible circumstances
I know that nothing is impossible with You.
I am utterly assured that:
In weakness or sickness
Catastrophe or anxiety
Loneliness or despair
I am Yours and You are mine.
Nothing can separate me
From Your matchless love!

GREATER THAN SIN

Lord, never before today
Have I so deeply understood
The ugliness of my sin.
But never before today
Have I been so completely submerged
In the ocean of Your grace.

AT THIS VERY MOMENT

O God
At this very moment
When I feel utterly abandoned
When I feel You are an enemy
And not my friend
When I feel You have turned Your face
And withdrawn Your love
At this very moment
I throw myself into Your arms
And stubbornly refuse to move.

What will You do with me now?

JUST COME HOME

God, You are so good!
When at last I called to You
From my prison without Exit
You did not exact from me
A solemn promise to do better.
You did not insist
That I adhere to an endless set of rules
To guarantee Your acceptance of me.
Nor did You say with frightening sternness
"Stand on your own two feet."
Rather, with breathtaking simplicity
You unlocked prison doors
You invaded the very depths of me

You encompassed me with transforming love.
On the very spot where I groped and grappled
You turned me about toward a rugged cross.
You pointed to an empty tomb.
Then with gentle urging You said
"Your past is obliterated
Your future is secure
Just come home!"

INSEPARABLE

One unforgettable day, dear God
You reached down to where I was
And lifted me up to where You are
And we have been inseparable
From that moment to this.

IT'S GOOD

God, it's good to be loved by You!
The breathtaking knowledge
Of Your life-giving love
Rings chimes in my tremulous heart.
It fashions eternal declarations
Out of unsettled questions.
It creates a majestic life symphony
From a solitary note.
God, it's good to be loved by You!

THE FACTS

Lord
When I feel I can't possibly make it
When I feel deluged with problems
When I feel helpless
Against the strange twistings of life
When I feel there is no way out
The FACT is
You have a Plan
You know what You're about.
The FACT is
The greater the strategy of the Enemy
The greater the assurance of victory.
The FACT is
The worst may seem to happen
But the best is on the way.
God, hold me to the facts.

FACTUAL

Lord
Not for a single moment
Could I make it
Down here
If You did not intercede for me
Up there.

BEAUTIFUL FACT

Lord
There are countless things in my life
That are inexcusable.
There are things unaccountable
And things unexplainable.
There are things irrefutable
And things irresponsible.
But it comes to me with unutterable relief
That because of Your amazing love
Nothing in my life is unforgivable.

IF IT IS TRUE

If it is true
As the speaker proclaimed
That You go to any ends
To bring harmony out of discord
And wholeness out of brokenness
Then, Lord
I may be in for a complete overhaul.

DESTINED

God, I am destined for You!
I was created for You!
Nothing I can ever do or think or feel

Can be separated from You.
With all my inner struggles
My self-absorption
My lethargy and fraud
I cannot alter to one degree
Your settled intention
Your divine purpose:
I was made to bring glory to You!

FINALLY—IMMEDIATELY

Lord
You said so gently
So persistently
"Give Me your weariness
And I'll give you My rest."
I did—finally.
You did—immediately.
Then, Lord, I marveled
That I had waited so long.

MARVELOUS MOMENTS

What a beautiful relief, dear God
To sit quietly in my own living room
Soaking up the luxury of aloneness.
No demanding voices
No radio or television

No shouts from the bathroom
Just these few marvelous moments
To kick off my shoes
Shed my confusion
And reclaim myself . . .
These few marvelous moments
To respond to Your persistent plea
"Be still and know that I am God."

COMMIT

Commit . . . commit . . . commit . . .
This is the word
That magnifies itself
In my struggling heart today.
Hold me tight, Lord.
Don't let me put my hands over my ears
To keep from hearing You.
May I do today
What lies luminously before me—
What I know I *must* do
If I am to awaken with peace tomorrow.

NOW

Lord
I don't ask You to renovate me
Nor do I ask You to reconstruct me

Or make me over.
I don't even ask You to patch me up
Or pare out the bruised spots
Or gloss over the tin and tarnish.
Rather, dear Lord, I ask You
To make a new species—
Something that never before existed.
Impart to me Your very own Life.
After all, Lord
It is such a simple thing for You
To create something beautiful
From a shapeless, chaotic mass.
It is such a simple thing for You
To divide light from darkness.
Please do it for me—now.

Child of My Infinite Plan
Two thousand years ago
All you have asked I did.
Please accept it from Me—now.

RIVERS AND RIVERS

O my Father
My heart longs for You!
Fill me to capacity with Your Spirit . . .
No, Father, I'm sorry—
That's not sufficient.
Fill me to *overflowing* with Your Spirit
And then increase my capacity

That there might be still more overflow.
Out of my life
May there flow rivers
And rivers
And still more rivers
Of Living Water
Bringing relief, release
And exhilarating refreshment
To a bruised and broken world
Where thirst can never be quenched
Apart from You.

SETTLED OBEDIENCE

God, I continue to discover
With growing insight
How utterly foolish it is
To ask what You want me to do
Unless I have resolved to do it.
My obedience must be settled
Regardless of how costly
How perplexing
How obviously difficult.
My obedience must come first
Unquestionably first
Before any pleasing or personal plan.
I am not called to be famous
I am called to be faithful.
I am not called to be recognized
I am called to be reconciled to You.

I am not called to be a celebrity
I am called to celebrate
The Reality of Jesus Christ.

ONE OF THE TWO

Dear God
Please help me.
I'm encumbered with problems
Too heavy to handle.

Dear child
Why should two of us
Carry the weight of your burden
When one of the two is Me?

RARE MOMENTS OF DELIGHT

Because You are God
And Your Word is unquestionable
There are things I assuredly know
Even when my heart is a brambled desert
And every ounce of emotion is drained:
I know Your love is everlasting
I know You will never forsake me
Nor will You leave me comfortless
I know I may come to You boldly
I know You will teach and instruct me

You will guide me with Your eye
I know my past is forgiven
And my future is secure.
But oh, dear God
How I praise You for the marvel
Of those rare, mysterious moments
When suddenly, without a flash or a sound
You add to my *knowing*
The ecstasy of *feeling*
And I am lifted to peaks of delight!

ALL THAT GLITTERS

I love our big church with its tall steeple
And impressive white pillars
You know I do, Lord.
But sometimes I get the impression
That we're running a sort of perpetual marathon
That keeps everyone gasping and gulping for
   breath.
Lord, I can't quite believe
You applaud all our frantic effort
Or demand each time-consuming activity
Or encourage our continual attempt
To function at galloping speed.

I wonder, dear Lord
Do statistics really matter so much?
Do our motives have more dross than silver?
Are we more eager to *do* than to *be?*

More anxious to impress than to reflect?
Would simplification increase
Rather than decrease our power?

So often, Lord
I feel trapped, drained, shattered
A living sacrifice to everyone but You.
When conferences and committee meetings
And car pools and exhausting rehearsals
Suck me in until I feel totally submerged
When status and glamour subtly urge me on
Then, Lord, I seem to hear You say:
"All that glitters is not God."

A BETTER WAY

A thousand times, dear Lord
In moments of fierce temptation
I have asked You to help me.
But at last I have learned a better way:
I no longer ask merely for help
I look up into Your gentle face
And ask You to do it all.

WORK ON ME

UNEXPECTED REPLY

Lord, dear Lord
I'm desperately pleading with You.
Please, please speak to my husband.
You see, he's made a determined decision
And I'm convinced he's totally wrong.
Change his mind, Lord.
Nudge him, prick him
Turn him around, anything—
But capture his attention
And show him I'm right.

*Foolish child, don't ask Me
To make your husband
What you want him to be.
Just ask Me to make him
What I want him to be.*

Oh, Lord . . .
Then You must work on me.

TRUSTING

Just this morning, Lord
As I dusted the living room furniture
I was thinking how variable my life is:
High moments and low moments
Deep joy, then when I least expect it
A crushing blow, a devastating loss

Until I feel ragged and wrung.
It happens like this again and again.
It happened today.
Do You want to explain it, Lord
Or must I just keep wondering?

Little one
Just keep trusting.

I KNOW WHO I AM

There he sat on his front porch
(Probably three or four years old)
And when he flashed a merry smile
I stopped to ask his name.
"I'm my daddy's boy," he said, grinning
And then he was off to play.
I still don't know his name, Lord
But it doesn't matter.
He knows who he is
And that makes everything all right.

Thank You, Lord
With all my heart
That I may say with genuine confidence
"I'm my Father's child."
That makes everything all right.

SPIRITUAL TUG-OF-WAR

Lord, I've waited long enough.
No longer can I withstand
This spiritual tug-of-war between us.
Today I will do what You asked me to do.
I still don't want to, Lord—
Surely You know that.
I'm frightened and ill-at-ease.
I feel foolish and uncomfortable.
I almost feel put-upon.
What You've asked of me slaps at my pride.
Nevertheless, I choose to obey You
Simply because I love You.
Do You understand, dear Lord?
I wouldn't do this
For anyone in the world—but You.

THE ANSWER

Lord
Sometimes Your answers come
With startling swiftness
Or sometimes the waiting is long . . .

Our friends with a fast-growing family
Consulted a realtor on Tuesday
And on Wednesday their house was sold.
Their hearts are full of praise to You.

Our friends four blocks from us
Are equally anxious to sell.
Their need for a larger house is urgent.
Six different times, dear Lord
Their dreams faded
As negotiations fell through.
Yet they are firmly convinced
That Your love encompasses
Every test and disappointment.
Their hearts are full of praise to You.

Thank You for both families
And for their authentic witness
To the power of praise—
When You say Yes
When You say No
When You say Wait.

WHEN I GROW UP

Hugging her tattered doll
Close to her tiny self
She asked persuasively
"Will you play house with me?
I'll be the mommie
You be the little girl."
So we played house.
We ate cookies and drank milk
With a napkin tucked under my chin.
We shopped in a make-believe store

And purchased a pretend-book.
We told stories, we asked riddles
We drew pictures with colored crayons.
After our imaginary nap she asked
"What do you want to be when you grow up?"
Before I could answer
Her friend Rachel knocked at our door
And I knew we would no longer play house.
But I haven't forgotten the question—
It repeats itself incessantly:
What do you want to be when you grow up?

When I grow up, dear Lord
I want to be as a little child
Trusting You, loving You, obeying You.
I want to walk with my hand in yours.
I want to laugh with you, cry with You
And share deep secrets with You.
I want to sit on Your lap
And listen to Your stories
With my head on Your shoulder.
Then at last
When I enter my Father's house
I want to hear You say
"My child, you have grown well
In grace and in knowledge
Of Jesus, your Lord.
Come, inherit the Kingdom prepared for you."
Then, dear Lord
I want to keep right on growing.

CHANGE ME

Change me, God
Please change me.
Though I cringe
Kick
Resist and resent
Pay no attention to me whatever.
When I run to hide
Drag me out of my safe little shelter.
Change me totally
Whatever it takes
However long You must work at the job.
Change me—and save me
From spiritual self-destruction.

MARRIAGE FORMULA

I read all these books on marriage
And sometimes I feel like a colossal failure.
I just don't always make it to the door
With a rosebud in my hair
When my husband comes home from work.
(After all, we have only one rosebush.)
I don't always remember to salt the eggs
Or pick up the suit from the cleaners
And often, too often
My mascara looks streaked.
But Lord, do You know what I pray for
Above all else in our marriage?

Just a walloping big heart of love—
A love that listens and understands
A love that accepts and forgives
A love that responds and trusts
And never once considers giving up.
Maybe that will make up for the rosebuds.

MY LIFE IS RICHER

How can I thank her, dear Lord
For what she did for me today.
How can I express my sudden release
Because she genuinely cared.
It was such a simple gesture, really—
A friendship card with a single line:
"My life is richer because of you."

You know, Lord, how numb I felt
Before the mail arrived.
Morning came much too soon
And I awakened weary, depleted.
For some unaccountable reason
Our house looked dismal and drab.
Most of the morning I berated myself
And fought a losing battle with doubt.
Then I heard the mailman.

O God, is it really true?
Is someone's life richer because of me?
Despite my whimpering

My defeats, my petty concerns
Am I usable in Your Kingdom, after all?
Suddenly, God, I believe that I am!

Forgive me for wasting a glorious morning
That should have been wrapped in praise.
Thank You especially for the friend
Who gathered my scattered emotions
And fused them into serenity
Without the slightest awareness of her mission.
Bless her abundantly, Lord
And please let her know
That *my* life is richer because of *her*.

SEEK FIRST

O Lord
How futile, how foolish
To attempt to keep up with the Joneses
On the gold-studded ladder of success.
Even if we make it
(Setting high, competitive goals)
We awake one dismal morning
To discover the Smiths have bypassed
   the Joneses
So it starts again—the goading competition.

God, Your objective is far more rewarding.
You want us to "keep up" with Your Plan
For our individual lives.

"Seek first the Kingdom of God"
Is Your shining word to us.
Forgive us for moments and days
(Even months)
When our love of money
Has exceeded our love for You.
Please, God
Be our Financial Advisor
And deliver us from a thousand "if onlys."
May we never be defeated
By the lack of money
Or captivated by the lure of it.

EXCLUSIVELY OURS

Through all the years of marriage
We've happily shared with others:
Our home, food, laughter, tears.
We've shared friendships and confidences
We've shared appreciation
We've shared music, books, flowers
We've shared victories and defeats.
But God, You've given us one priceless gift
That belongs exclusively to us
Not to be shared with another—
The beautiful gift of physical intimacy.
Thank You for its mystery
Its wonder, its delight.
May we never mishandle it.
May we respect and cherish it always.

May our self-giving continue to be
An expression of oneness
A celebration of wholeness.
Keep it alive, fulfilling
And always full of surprises.
O God, what a marvelous expression
Of Your own fathomless love!

THIS TIME

Hesitantly she asked
"Will you pray for me?"
Lord, her troubled, tear-filled eyes
Have haunted me ever since.
Oh, she is so young, so beautiful
And on her college campus
The walls against conviction stand so erect.
She is tortured by the knowledge
Of the reality of her guilt
But her struggle with temptation
Seems intolerable at times.
It comes, she said, in rhythmic waves.
It dazes, it taunts, it baffles her.

Speak to her tormented heart, Lord.
Comfort her, sustain and strengthen her.
Assure her of Your enabling power
To steady her against future assaults.
Help her to cling tenaciously
To an inescapable fact:

"No degree of temptation
Justifies any degree of sin."
You Yourself have promised
An immediate way of escape—
All the time
Every time
This time.

LOUD AND CLEAR

Through years of Sundays
I've listened to preachers
Who love to preach.
But one refreshing Sunday, Lord
I listened to a preacher
Who loved those to whom he preached.
Your message came through loud and clear.

DEFENSELESS

There I was, Lord
A half-block from church
My Bible under my arm
The hymns still ringing in my ears
The sermon fresh in my thoughts . . .
There I was
Sharply reprimanding my young son
For not scrubbing his ears.

His answer left me defenseless:
"At least God washed my heart."

TRANSFORMATION

Lord
I have studied
I have prepared
I have prayed.

Now, as I teach my class
This lovely Sunday morning
Fill me with Your love
Your radiance
Your wisdom and power.
Make my life the proof
Of the truth I proclaim.

I am not content, dear Lord
Simply to impart information.
I long to behold transformation.

SAD SUBSTITUTE

Lord
This opinionated man
Now leading our Bible study
Is so insistent

So dogmatic and explosive
It begins to seem
He has ceased to believe in You
And believes instead
In his own beliefs.
What a sad substitute!

POINT OF VIEW

Really, Lord
Wasn't my dress a tremendous bargain?
Frankly, I haven't seen such a sale
In a good many months.
If only my dear practical husband
Weren't always so practical.
He admired the dress
And then he bluntly questioned me
About our promised church pledge.
I justified my purchase
And skirted around the pledge talk.
(I plan to make it up next month, Lord.)
I wasn't at all prepared
For my husband's quiet comment:
"What's God's point of view?"

Lord
Now what'll I do?

IN A SUPERMARKET

Today I pushed a wobbly cart
Down the wide aisles of a supermarket.
I was one of a crowd of women
Who were strangers to each other.
Nobody knew my name
There was no one whose name I knew.

I stopped by the soup section
And picked up three cans of tomato soup.
The woman next to me chose celery soup.
We smiled slightly
Mumbled something about rising costs
And went our individual ways.
All we shall ever know of each other
Is that one of us bought tomato soup
The other cream of celery.

But Lord
You know *everything* about us both.
You know our every thought.
You were there while we were formed
In utter seclusion.
You scheduled our days and our years.
You are constantly thinking about us—
About her, Lord
About me.

Whoever she is, whatever her name
I pray for the woman
Who bought cream of celery soup.
How precious she is to You.
O God, may she know!

IT TAKES WORK

Brown eyes
Shiny hair
Blue jeans and sweater
Ten years old . . .

It was an excellent piano lesson
And I happily told her so.
Then I teasingly asked
"How did it happen?"
Her response was half-smiling
Half-indignant:
"It didn't just happen—I worked!"
What beautiful reassurance, Lord
Especially today—
Our wedding anniversary.
A positive vital marriage
Never just happens.
It takes renewed motivation
It takes commitment
It takes determination
It takes stupendous effort
It takes work!

CONTINUAL DISCOVERY

Dear Lord
It sings in me again and yet again—
The ever-expanding joy, the fulfillment
Of living with my gentle husband.

For thirty-three years
He's thrown stardust in my eyes
And flowers in my path.
Just this morning I found a love note
Taped to the mirror in our bathroom
And one day last week he called to say
"In case you've forgotten, I love you!"

Through stumbling and victories
Through laughter and tears
We continue to discover
We're so right for each other.
Only You, dear Lord
Could have given so great a gift.

FASTIDIOUS HOUSEKEEPER

O God
She is such a fastidious housekeeper
Every day she cleans and cleans—
Every crack, every corner
Including the picture hangers on the walls.
She insists it simply has to be done
But when I see her lonely husband
So obviously frustrated
So totally shelved
I wish there were some way
To convince her to include him
In her cleaning schedule.
Lord, he needs dusting off too.

OUR BEAUTIFUL NEW CAR

There it stands in our driveway—
Our beautiful new car.
(Well, I guess two years old
Isn't exactly new
But at least it's newer
Than any car we've ever had.)
How excited we are, Lord
How thankful for Your sure guidance.
You enabled us to sell our old car
You directed us in the financial plan
And now You are flooding our hearts
With enough genuine optimism
To call the car "ours"
Though we have twenty payments to make!

MISTAKEN VALUES

Forgive me, Lord!
Every day last week
I sat at the kitchen table
Dawdling away an hour
Over a cup of instant coffee
Without giving a solitary thought
To Your eternal Word.

THE CHALLENGE

It may be true, dear God
That my husband and I had more to live on
A year ago than we have today
But it is equally true
That we have just as much to live *for*.
The real values of our lives remain
Solid, stable, unshifting.
Our financial loss has in no way
Diminished the value of a single friendship.
We have lost nothing of human dignity
And we are discovering spiritual realities
Full of wonder and sheer delight.
Our faith in Your loving kindness
Adds growing serenity to our guided lives.
You are making us increasingly aware
That what we *are* is vastly more vital
Than our fondest possessions.
Above all, You are teaching us
That a limited salary is our shining challenge
To trust and exalt our limitless God!

WHY
DIDN'T I THINK
OF THAT?

SOLUTION

Today, after hours of praying
For something that didn't come
Something I so desperately craved
I see anew, dear God
That with all my clamoring
And agonized pleading
I simply cannot change You.

No, dear child
But I can change you.

THE REASON

God, why am I so often defeated?
Why am I so full of dread and anxiety?
Why am I so lamentably weak—
So perilously susceptible to temptation?
Why am I often inhospitable
So intolerant of the needs of others?
Why am I so undisciplined
So restless and dissatisfied?
Why do I protest so violently?
Above all, God
Why do I so frequently lose
The sense of Your shining Presence?
God, why?
Why?

"Because you pray so little."

ABOVE ALL

O Lord, my God
May I fear nothing
As much as I fear sin.
May I love no one
As much as I love You.

HE CAN BE TRUSTED

If You, dear God
Could entrust
To Jesus, your Son
The salvation of the world
Throughout all eternity
Then surely I can entrust
To Jesus, my Savior
The solution to my problem
Today.

IN TOUCH

"And Enoch walked
In constant touch with God."

Lord
The best news of all is—
That which was possible for Enoch

Is possible for me.
Today
Tomorrow
Forever
In constant touch with God.
Me.

Indescribable joy!

PRECIOUS TREASURE

O dear Lord
How can You know all about me—
Everything I've ever done—
And still love me so extravagantly?
You treat me as if I were
A precious treasure or something.
The beautiful part is—
To You I am!

TOO SLEEPY

When I awoke this morning
You said so clearly
"Don't worry about anything
Instead, pray about everything . . . "
So, dear Lord, all day long

Will You keep me so prayerfully occupied
With Your assigned tasks
That I will find no time to worry.
Then tonight, when I finally lie down
And stretch out on my comfortable bed
Please silence my clamoring thoughts
And make me too sleepy to worry.

FORGIVE ME

Lord
So often I am
Fearful
Unbelieving
And apologetic about my faith.
I analyze
Whittle down
And tear apart
Your very words.
I conjure foolish reasons
For my lack of trust
As though You couldn't possibly mean
What You so clearly said.
Yet, all the while You wait for me
To believe *exactly* what You said—
Without exception
Without alteration.
Forgive me for treating You
Like someone who would lie.

I TRY

Lord
Never in a million years
Could I adequately thank You
For Your amazing goodness
Your matchless love—
But I like to try!

THE ONLY THING

Thank You, thank You, God
For creating within me
An intense and powerful longing
For You . . .
You . . .
You . . .
Success doesn't matter anymore, Lord.
Rich or poor
Recognized or nameless
Win or lose
The only thing that matters
The *only* thing, dear Lord
Is to walk hand-in-hand
And heart-to-heart with You.
Nothing in my life
Has any real or lasting significance
Unless it relates to You.

INCREDIBLY REWARDING

Early this morning, Lord
I read Your solemn words:
"If anyone wants to follow
In my footsteps he must
Give up all right to himself."
All this long day I have been
Thinking, pondering, reflecting.
Lord, You make it incredibly difficult.

Yes, my child
And incredibly rewarding.

GIFT EXCHANGE

Dear God
This Christmas
I want to give You me.
I come just as I am
Unboxed
Unribboned
Without glitter
Or glamour.
On the name tag of my heart
I've written
"To God with love."
Do with me exactly as you choose.

Dear child
I choose to give you Me.

OVERWHELMED

All day long, dear God
I have been overwhelmed
With my failure
And folly.
Now please overwhelm me
With Your faithfulness
And forgiveness.

TRY ME

O Lord
Is there anyone
In all the world
Who really understands me?

*Yes, dear child
Me.*

WHY IN THE WORLD?

When I complained
"I just can't do it"
Your response was immediate:
"Of course not.
That's why you have Me."

Lord, why in the world
Didn't I think of that?

FAILURE

Sometimes, God
I feel like a failure
In everyone's sight but Yours.

Dear child
Be glad it isn't reversed.

I TRUST YOU

O God, I trust You.
I don't understand
I cannot begin to comprehend
The wisdom of Your way
In my torn and tangled life
But I am steadfastly believing
That Your plan for me today
Must be—
Surely it *must* be
As kind
As loving
As profitable
As Your plan for me
In joyful days now past.

You are the same
Yesterday
And today
And forever
So, dear God
I trust You.

ONCE AND FOR ALL

Lord
May I settle it once and for all
That I am dealing directly with You.
You need never apologize
For any plan You ordain for me
Since nothing but good
Can come from Your hand.
You are sufficient
For every *changing* circumstance
In my God-planned life—
For every *unchanging* circumstance as well.

DISCOVERIES

Lord God
Today You have penetrated
My entire being
With three glorious discoveries:
When I am most weak

You are most strong.
When I am most fearful
You are utterly faithful.
When I am at my sinning worst
You are at Your saving best.

WHICH, LORD?

Lord
I always seem to be
The child in Your family
Who needs the most chastening.
Is it because
I'm so unmanageable
Or is it because
You love me so much?

YOU DID ALL THE REST

O Lord God!
I did what You asked me to do:
I just opened windows
Wide . . .
Wide . . .
And You did all the rest!
You poured into my heart
A blessed, blissful contentment.
You saturated my mind

With gigantic thoughts of You.
You struck an artesian well within me
Until sheer joy sprang forth.
You led me out of the valley of despair
Into a succession of incredible happenings.
Problems which seemed insurmountable
Melted like wax before my eyes.
Fears faded away like threatening clouds.
You startled me
You amazed me
With the glory of Your revelation.
It is true
Gloriously true—
I have literally walked and breathed with God.
I just opened windows
Wide . . .
Wide . . .
God, You did all the rest!

USABLE

Lord, this is one of those "blob days"
When I feel useless and ineffective.
Somehow, I feel totally unrelated
To a world of people who need You.
I hear preachers, talented musicians
And women who speak at luncheon clubs
Whose Christian witness excites and challenges.
Hundreds of lives are changed, renewed
Because of their dynamic message.

I too want to live for You radiantly.
I want to be Your instrument
In motivating and revitalizing others.
But nothing I do seems to reach very far.
To tell the truth, I feel quite unnecessary.
Did I miss Your instructions
Or is there nothing for me to do?

Fretting child
I did not call you to flaunt your talents
I called you to serve me sincerely
Where, when, and how I choose.
If you are usable, you will be used.
It is to your great spiritual advantage
That you don't know to what extent.

EMPOWER ME, I PRAY

Lord, You told the impotent man
To take up his bed and walk.
Today, when mountainous problems
Seem to loom sky-high
And the business of living
Demands so much rigid attention
Empower me, I pray
To take up my task and work.

PROBLEMS, NOT BATTLES

Help me, Lord.
Too often
I see mounting pressures
As battles to be won
Rather than problems to be solved.

DON'T YOU UNDERSTAND?

But Lord
Don't You understand?
If I can't, I *can't!*

*But child
Don't you understand?
If I can, I can!
Things which are
Impossible with you
Are possible with Me.*

DIGGING DEEP

WHAT'S MYSELF DOING TO MYSELF?

With childish intensity she asked
"What's myself doing to myself?"
I couldn't help but smile
As she stood before the mirror
Struggling so impatiently
With a stubborn jacket zipper.

But I'm not smiling now, Lord
As I pass my own mirror
And glance at the tension
Etching my somber face.
I'm frightened, Lord.
Her innocent question clutches me:
"What's myself doing to myself?"

Frustrated, frantic
So often breathless
Too many irons in the fire . . .
What am I doing to my body—
To my mind, my emotions?
What am I doing to my family?
What am I doing to Your Plan
For my personal fulfillment?
Why do I live like this, Lord
As though Your world
Couldn't exist without me?
Why do I so often
Tear myself from Your control?

Dear Lord, calm me.
Pull me off the merry-go-round

Of converging conflicts.
Give balance to my boggled mind.
This very hour, Lord
Infuse me with Your poise and power
Until my total self
Is submerged in You—Yourself.
Only then will I be free
To be myself.

HOW SHALL I PRAY FOR THEM?

O dear God
How desperately I ache for them.
They are like frightened children
Lost in a dense and wooded forest.

Through bitter sobs she told me
That she had never felt so desolate
So utterly devoid of hope—
That life seemed futile, useless
That all her dreams had crashed
Like crystal goblets
Flung against jagged rocks.

With guarded caution he told me
That life had become
An intolerable drudgery
That year after weary year
He had met with cynical indifference
That never had he felt significant
In all his years of marriage.

O Lord
Whatever the deep-seated implications
Love has been strangled
And lives have been mangled—
Leaving nothing but twisted rubble.
How shall I pray for them, God?
What shall I ask?
Perhaps this above all:
That out of their failure and hurt
Their gloom and despair
They might sense their need of You—
The Redeemer of all their Yesterdays
And the Answer to all their Tomorrows!

SHAPING THE WORLD

God, I so long for our small house
To be a sacred shrine, without shadow or snare.
Cleanse me, I pray, from divided loyalties
From destructive attitudes
From anxiety and self-pity.

I need so much an enlightened grasp
Of my husband's responsibilities
That I might pray with increased wisdom.
Support my determination to read, to learn
As together we pursue intellectual interests.
May I accept my husband's preferences
Without unreasonable protest.

When opinions clash, make me willing
  to compromise
At least some of the time.

Above all, dear God
Remind me often of my need for undisturbed
    prayer
If I am to confront each day with cheerful poise.
Please, Lord, keep me jubilant in You.
May I demonstrate Your enormous love
In every smile, every touch, every apple pie.
Revitalize my youthful honeymoon intent
To make our small home a kind of "Haven of
    Rest."

Then, Lord
Day by day, year after year
Will You remind us both
That we have a share in shaping the world
In our town
On our street
In a small yellow house
With glistening white trim.

YOUR WORD TO ME

*The Word of the Lord which came
unto Zephaniah . . .*

Lord, how incredible!
Neither Shakespeare nor Browning

Nor Shelley nor Keats
Would have dared to speak with such blunt
  boldness.

But God, in Your infinite wisdom
In Your exquisite Plan
You personally chose to express Yourself
Through obscure and ordinary men
Like Ezra and Micah
Like Moses and Zephaniah.
Centuries ago they heard You:
Sometimes in an open field
Or on a wind-swept hill.
Sometimes at the break of dawn
Or under a star-filled sky.
Through sorrow and suffering
Through tumult and war
In peace and in prosperity
Ancient voices, directed by Your Spirit
Sublimely proclaimed Your spoken Word.

Now today, when I open the Book of books
I too hear You speak.
Sometimes as I sit at my desk
Or on a kitchen stool.
Sometimes at the table
Or on the living room floor.

Me, Lord!
So ordinary!
So obscure!
From the pages of Your sacred Word

The God of the Universe speaks to me.
How incredible!

I FELT LED

Forgive me, Lord, for so often
Hiding under the protective covering
Of the words, "I felt led."
How convenient the phrase becomes—
How comforting
How soothing.
I've resorted to "I felt led"
When errors in judgment have betrayed me
When pride has swallowed me whole.
Under the subtle guise of "I felt led"
I've spent money recklessly
I've lashed out unmercifully
I've neatly evaded responsibility.

But today, Lord, I'm disturbed.
I've heard Your convicting voice
Persuading me that I dare not
Ride slipshod over others
In determining Your will.
I must seek Your guidance honestly
Without taking shortcuts
Or zooming in with push-button answers
Or kneeling on a cushion of "I felt led."
Teach me God-reliance, not self-reliance.
Above all, in seeking guidance

May I focus all my attention
On You, my Guide.

OH, HOW WE PRAISE YOU, GOD

Oh, how we praise You, God
For the marvel of our differences.
I am a woman—
First and foremost a woman.
I have a woman's understanding
A woman's discernment and empathy
A woman's emotional response.
My husband is a man—
First and foremost a man.
He has a man's practicality
A man's logic and perception
A man's ambition.
Equal in value and dignity?
Assuredly!
Nevertheless, we function differently.
We express differently
We react differently.
"Male and female created he them."
This fact we cannot change
Nor do we want to.
Oh, how we praise You, God
For the marvel of our differences
And for the wisdom of Your plan.

IS THAT WRONG?

Her hurt reaches deep, so deep.
She is lonely and full of longing
And when she awakens in the morning
She often wishes that night had just begun.
One day she said, tears streaming her face
"I love the old song about telling Jesus alone
But sometimes I wish that *just once*
I could tell my husband, too."
Then she asked pensively
"Is that wrong?"
No, God, no!
It is very right.
But how to convince her husband?

I HAVE A FATHER

Lord, it was one humdinger of a fight.
I wondered if it would ever end.
But three solid blows later
Little Loser limped toward his home.
With his fists clenched, he shouted:
"I'll tell my father on you!"
(I had a feeling he meant it.)
Then all of a sudden it happened—
Out the front door he walked
Calm and serene
His tall hefty father by his side.
Like a streak of jagged lightning
His frightened opponent was on the run.

O Lord, what a reflection of me.
I too must do battle
With the adversary of my soul.
At times he comes masked
As an angel of light.
He thwarts and antagonizes.
He blinds and binds.
He harasses and accuses.
I'm no match for him, Lord.
The battle wages against
Principalities and powers.

But the great triumphant truth is—
I have a Father.
My Father protects and upholds me.
He strengthens and supports me.
Nothing can happen to me
Outside my Father's will.
My Father is greater by far
Than he who is in the world.
Once and for all it was settled
On a rugged cross
On a lonely hill:
I have a Father.

HIS PART—MY PART

Lord
You want me to trust You so totally
That I am unmoved by any circumstance:

Then work in me that steadfast trust.
You want me to choose to do right:
Then turn me from wanting any plan but Yours.
You want me to revere and honor You:
Then refresh and revive me.
You want me to obey You uninterruptedly:
Then make Your Word my guide.
You want me to depend upon You increasingly:
Then reassure me that Your promises are mine.
You want Your will to be my will:
Then help me to love Your every wish.

I expect Your help, dear Lord
For You've never broken a single promise
And You're not going to start with me.

I AM

Lord, I've never identified with Moses
As much as I do today.
When You gave him a stupendous task
He told You he was the wrong man.
He had never been a speaker
And he never would be, he insisted . . .

In just an hour from now
I'll be stuttering and stammering
Before a group of talented women
Who will undoubtedly smile
At my obvious awkwardness.

For the first time in my life
I'm about to give a devotional message
And my legs feel like apple jelly.
Lord, I said Yes for one reason:
I honestly thought You were nudging me—
I thought You were encouraging me.
Now, however, I question my own insight.
I am so common, so ordinary, so insignificant
Your servant Moses had nothing on me.

Frightened one, just trust Me.
As I was with Moses, so I am with you.
I am going to take the most common thing
The most ordinary thing
The most insignificant thing in your life
And make it powerful in my service.
This very day—I AM.

PRODIGAL DAUGHTER

Again, dear Lord
I pray for the dear distraught mother
Who called me early this morning.
Thoughts of her keep hovering
And I feel thrust into the midst
Of her fear and bewilderment.

In a tense and turbulent scene
Her daughter shouted with savage anger:
"I don't care what you say—

I'll never come home, never!"
And now the mother is torn and tortured
With the bitter memory
Of clashing wills and crushing words.
She maligns herself relentlessly, Lord.
She wonders if she risked too much
Or denied too much
Or gave too much.
Perhaps she was too lenient
Or at times too harsh
Or too often absorbed in her own interests.
Over and over she rehashes it.

O God
With all her gnawing guilt
Help her to see
That none of her blundering questions
Will bring her daughter home.
She needs to turn her thoughts
From her blunders to Your blessings—
From her despair to Your deliverance.
Though her dreams lie lifeless
Enable her even now to trust You.
Touch her songless heart with hope
And remind her often, Lord
That when You spoke of the Prodigal Son
You meant a daughter, too.

CONSOLATION

He is old.
His hair is silver-white.
Day after day
For eight dreary months
He walked from his home
To the hospital six blocks away.
Day after day
He sat by her bedside
Gently stroking her feeble hand.
Only occasionally did she recognize him
Or know he was there.
But when she responded
With just a trace of a smile
Tears of elation filled his shadowed eyes.

A week ago Tuesday
He walked to the hospital
For the last time.
Had she lived but one more week
They would have observed
Their sixtieth wedding anniversary.

Until You take him, Lord
May his own consoling words
Be his great sustaining force:
*"We've had longer together
Than we'll ever have apart."*

WHAT MORE COULD A MOTHER ASK?

Lord, with all my heart I thank You
For a trusting teenager
Who is sufficiently secure and mature
To seek parental guidance.

Last night she approached me directly:
"Mom, I've got a real problem
And I need to share it with you."
For over an hour we talked
(As we've often done before)
Personally
Intimately
With beautiful freedom
With healthy objectivity.
All the while I prayed for direction.
I knew You had given it, Lord
When suddenly she grabbed my hand
Sighed deeply
And said with obvious relief:
"Thanks, Mom. You've helped.
I sort of knew you would."

Then this morning
After she'd dashed out the door
I found her hurriedly-scribbled note:
"Mom: You're like a personal rainbow
After a storm.
Thanks—and a whole bunch of love."

Dear Lord
What more could a mother ask?

WHICH PART OF HIM WENT TO
HEAVEN?

Lord . . . dear Lord
Which part of him went to heaven?
My heart cries out to know.
Was it his laughing eyes?
His sandy hair?
His boyish grin?
But, Lord—
I saw them put that part of him
Far, far beneath the black earth.

Was it his awareness, Lord?
That part of him
That chose blue ties
And rare steaks
And symphonies?
Even that part that
Worried
Struggled
Dreamed?
Perhaps—
But his blue ties look drab
As they hang without life
And symphonies sound like funeral songs.

O dear Lord
I so long to know:
Which part of him went to heaven?

Was it his intense conviction?
His secret longings?
The challenges he so nobly accepted?

Was it his ever-deepening belief
That life has significance—
That You are total Reality?

Please tell me, Lord—
Which part of him went to heaven?

"I will . . . receive you unto myself; that where I
    am, there ye may be also" (John 14:3).

PRACTICE LOVING

It is so simple, dear Lord
So pleasant and comfortable
To sit in church on a Sunday morning
Listening to a sermon about love—
Perhaps even speculating a bit
On whether my love surpasses the love
Of the person to my right
Or the person to my left.
But to love with Your love
To practice loving, dear God
How uncomfortable the church pew becomes
When I hear this ringing challenge
When I see Your gazing eyes.
Suddenly I remember the vicious remarks
Of the woman who misjudged me.
I remember the unscrupulous associate
Who finagled my husband's job.
I remember the careless driver

Who totaled our shining new car.
So quickly, Lord, I am faced
With a haunting parade
Of shameful, unloving attitudes.
God, You know me so much better
Than I know my own complex self
And still You continue to love me.
Give me, I pray, a fresh glimpse
Of Your vast, immeasurable love
For it is only out of gratitude for Your love
That I shall finally learn
What it means to practice loving.

GOD'S SEARCHLIGHT

O God
If suddenly You were to reveal
To my family, my friends, my neighbors
Every real thought behind my courteous words
If You were to point to my clenched fist
While my other hand is openly extended
If You were to bring to light
Every masked motive, every selfish act
I would cringe with remorse
And beg You to remove Your light of revelation.
Yet, Lord, when the searchlight of the Holy Spirit
Begins to reveal me to *myself*
I so often close my eyes and turn my back
In a frantic but impossible effort
To escape Your penetrating gaze.

What a staggering contradiction, Lord
What appalling hypocrisy.
Apart from Your grace I am utterly shattered.
I ask You to sweep through me
Purify me, cleanse me completely.
From the depth of my penitent heart
I thank You for your continual assurance
As I turn toward Your splintered cross:
Because of Your love I *became* Your child
Because of Your grace I *remain* Your child.

NEW BIBLE

This was an exciting day for me, Lord!
This morning I opened my new Bible.
Not a single word was circled
Not a single phrase underlined.
Now with each new day
I can circle and underline again
I can word-clutter the margins
And I know what will happen, Lord—
I'll be asking as I read
Why didn't I see that before?
But even with the joy of a new Bible
I'm going to miss my old one
With its tattered pages—
Its creased and torn edges.
Oh, how many personal notes
Are jotted on the margins
How many God-whispered secrets.

Yes, Lord, I'll miss it.
But thank You for a friend's reminder:
"If your Bible is falling apart
Chances are your life isn't."

LORD,
REMIND ME OFTEN

LORD, REMIND ME OFTEN TODAY

Lord, remind me often today . . .

That if there is some area in my life
Not fully surrendered to You
That is always the area
In which I will be most severely tried.

Lord, remind me often today . . .

That You've already done Your part:
You've provided a way of escape
Against every temptation I shall face.
I must *choose* Your escape-door.

Lord, remind me often today . . .

That You want more than first place
In my heart and life.
You want all of me, always.
Surrender means every detail of my life
Under your careful scrutiny.

Lord, remind me often today . . .

That You alone are my Source.
Only God
Always God
Totally God
You alone are my Source.

EMBARRASSED

I was terribly embarrassed, Lord
I could feel my face turn crimson.
I sat at a luncheon table
With three sophisticated women
Expounding with great flourish
On the content of a current book.
But when one of the women asked who wrote it
I totally forgot the author.

Dear child
Let this be a quiet reminder
Of how prone you are
To expound on your own life
While totally forgetting your Creator.

ALL THE WAY

Lord, now that the dishes are done
And the kitchen is clean and shiny
I just want to thank You personally
For our special dinner guests
And for our rewarding evening of sharing.
How exciting it was, Lord
How challenging and inspiring
To sit at our candle-lit table
With the charming couple
Who have so recently met You.

The glowing words of the beautiful wife
Still throb in my grateful heart:
"God changed me—changed me all the way
From alcohol to attitudes."
O God, bless this radiant couple
As they learn to know You better.
Through Your own transforming Word
Continue to change them all the way
From Genesis to Revelation.

EXACTLY NOTHING

Sometimes, Lord, I feel restless
Just plain empty
And I secretly begin to wonder
If everything I say
Everything I write
Is just a lot of nothing
Scattered here and there—
A lot of nothing You could do without.
Then I remember Your startling words
"Without Me you can do nothing"
And I see with gnawing remorse
That my futile nothings are always the result
Of my foolish attempts to make it on my own.
Thank You for convicting me
For deliberately pulling me back
And for reminding me in many pricking ways
That my contribution apart from You
Is always the same—exactly nothing.

UNTIL SHE IS WILLING

Please, dear God
Assure her of my loving concern.
Help her to know I care for her
And genuinely long to befriend her
But she is so frantically fretful
So steeped in self-pity
That any suggestion I casually make
Seems only to flame her hostility.

God, I want to understand her limitations.
Guard me against being cheaply cheerful.
I'll walk with her eagerly toward health
No matter how steep the climb
Or how prolonged the effort.
I'll listen to her, pray with her
But until she is willing to change
I can no longer be her crutch.
She grasps so intensely
I sometimes feel strangled.
The more heavily she leans
The more locked-in she becomes.

Lord, I know only one thing to do:
I release her completely to You.
Speak to her festering heart
Find *some* way of letting her know
That You alone are her Answer—
You have no competitor.
Show her, dear God
That she'll never be free to step out
Until she asks You to step in.

I WILL BE PLEASED

Lord, this fresh early morning
As I sit in our quiet living room
You've just reminded me
Through David the Psalmist
That there is incomparable joy
For those who delight to please You—
For those who are thinking about ways
To follow You more closely.
Lord, the day stretches out before me.
In a few brief moments I must arouse my family
And face again the noise, the distraction
The hubbub of confusion.
But while we are still alone
Just the two of us, my Lord
While Your peace floods my tranquil heart
Please tell me what I can do
This duty-packed day
To follow You more closely.

Dearly-loved child
Praise me joyfully
Talk with me intimately
Trust me totally
And I will be pleased.

SPIRITUAL DILEMMA

The Apostle Paul said it first, Lord
In his letter to the Romans:
"For we do not know how to pray as we ought."
This morning my anxious heart echoes his words.
My thoughts have trudged miles of misery.
I am terribly confused, exhausted
And my husband is, too.
We want so much to do Your will
But first we must *know* Your will.
We've done everything we know how to do:
We've read and studied Your Word
We've sought the advice of mature Christians
We've written a list of "pros and cons"
One dismal day we even fasted as we prayed.

Still we feel pulled and pushed, Lord.
We vascillate without settled peace.
To us it is such a momentous decision.
Should we take this gigantic step or not?
Perhaps Your direct word to us is simply: Wait.
But time is limited and our endurance is, too.
Calm us, quiet us, Lord.
At times we are such stupid children.
Give us teachable minds.
Give us listening hearts.

Thank You, Lord, for Paul's added message:
"The Spirit himself intercedes for us
With sighs too deep for words."
Right now I stretch my total being
On the assurance of this changeless fact.

I come to You like the little child
Who simply "prayed" the alphabet from A to Z.
May the Holy Spirit arrange the letters.

AN ECHO

God, may I never be content
To be but the echo
Of my environment.
Empower me day by day
To be the echo
Of Your amazing love
In my God-guarded life!

YOU CANNOT BE HID

Lord, I've discovered it's never a secret
When You live in a home
For You simply cannot be hid.
The neighbors soon know You are there
Even strangers learn of Your presence.
When You are the Great First in a home
There is a radiance that speaks of joy
There is gentleness, kindness
Laughter and love.
There is commotion mixed with contentment
There are problems mixed with prayer.
Lord, Your own Word says it so vividly:
"It was known that He was in the house."

LORD, MAKE ME AWARE

Lord, make me aware of . . .
Sunlight filtering through the trees
The song of the March wind
Crickets at twilight
Water splashing in soapsuds
Yellow daffodils in a crystal vase
Delicate china on pink mats
The aroma of fresh coffee
The first day of spring
Green peas and red beets
A dewdrop on a rose
Freckles on a grinning face
The longing in my husband's eyes.

BOOK OF ALL BOOKS

Lord, I am overwhelmed
As I read Your living Word.
What power, what pungency
I find within its pages.
It stirs me, burns within me
It challenges me, invigorates me
And often disturbs me.
When I obey its commands
The results are what You claim:
Darkness becomes light
Crooked places become straight
The more I seek, the more I find.

Within its pages, God
I see beyond mere philosophy
I see beyond a neat package of ethics.
I crash head-on with a living Person
The One who makes all things new.
No other book can claim as much.

INCREASE MY ENTHUSIASM

Lord, with gratitude
And genuine enthusiasm
I pray for those who love me.
But I must ask You now
To increase my enthusiasm
As I pray for those who don't.

IN YOUR NAME I CLAIM

O Lord God
I am so weary tonight
I cannot formulate a single thought.
All I can do is pronounce Your Name
Over every concern
Every need
Every one dear to my heart—
And in Your all-powerful Name
I claim all!

I CAN STILL BELIEVE

I don't know why, dear God—
I simply cannot interpret
The sudden changes
That have come into my life
Nor can I explain the awful anguish
The crushing disappointment.
But, God, I can still believe
That You always bring ultimate good
To those who love You
And Lord, You *know* that I love You.

IT DOESN'T MATTER AT ALL

I was scrubbing the kitchen floor today
When two friends came by unexpectedly.
I know I looked awful when I opened the door
But suddenly, Lord, Your Word came flashing:
"Be given to hospitality."
So we laughed and chatted
I served hot tea in delicate cups
And hoped I was covering my embarrassment.
Oh well, Lord
I guess it doesn't matter very much
When I'm caught unawares
If Your love shines through.

Dear child
It doesn't matter at all.

YOU LOVE ME

Yesterday, God, I was soaring
Like a graceful eagle
And You loved me.
Today I feel like a blob
And You love me.
Tomorrow I may ask
"Whatever happened
To disturb me yesterday?"
And You'll love me.

God, there are innumerable things
I cannot begin to comprehend
But the one great certainty
In all my life is this:
I know that You love me.

TWO BEAUTIFUL PARENTS

O dear Lord
I can never sufficiently thank You
For two beautiful parents
Who loved me into loving You.
Who praised me
Corrected me
Forgave me
And unwaveringly believed in me.
Who nurtured me
Nursed me back to health

And unceasingly prayed for me.
Who laughed with me
Cried with me
Comforted me
Rejoiced with me.
I know You better
Far better, Lord
Because of their authentic lives.
Thank You!

NEED OF PATIENCE

O God
How pointedly You speak to my heart
When You say, "You have need of patience . . ."
Remorsefully I acknowledge Your truth
For there is nothing I need more.
I am so easily disturbed, Lord
So many little things annoy me.
Patience is simply not a virtue of mine.

I'm impatient with our neighbor
Who mows his lawn but once every six weeks.
I'm impatient with our newsboy
Every time he misses our front porch.
Yesterday a friend kept me waiting
And I robed my impatience in self-pity.

Shoes pushed under the bed
An unrinsed coffee cup

An overly-detailed story
Toys scattered on our lawn—
How I murmur and fret.
(Sometimes I explode.)

I'm impatient with myself, Lord
My foolish mistakes, my failures
And often I'm impatient with You.
I am like a petulant child
Who insists on an answer—*now*.

Yes, God, I have need of patience.
But I will not be discouraged
Nor will I continue to flog myself.
Again Your Word speaks pointedly:
"My God shall supply all your need . . . "
The very need You know I have
Is the very need You will supply.
You will renew me in patience.
In You there is hope!

THE GARDEN

THE GARDEN

Lord
There was a time
When I felt so small
So empty and forlorn
I saw myself
As nothing more
Than a tiny speck—
Worthless at that.
But You picked me up
And planted me in rich soil.
Then You whispered softly:
"You shall be like a watered garden
Bearing much fruit."
I must have value after all.
Why else would You choose
A tiny speck?

One thing is sure—
The garden will tell!

I WILL LET YOU

Early this morning, Lord
An hour or so before dawn
You whispered a secret
Within my trembling heart . . .

You said, "If you will let me
I will make this seeming tragedy

The most valuable experience
Of your entire life.
I will blaze a luminous trail
Through the vast wilderness.
Where there is sand and tumbleweed
I will cultivate a fertile valley.
I will plant green trees by still waters
If you will let Me."

O Lord, Yes!
I will let You!

SO PROFOUND

O God
I want to sing and dance
I want to shout it from the hilltops:
There is absolutely nothing
In my wretched past
That can hinder You
From redeeming my future
Except my refusal to let You.
Thank You for invading my heart
With a truth so refreshing
So magnificent
So profound!

YOU DREAMED ME UP

O dear God
It was You, You alone
Who dreamed me up.
Nobody else
Would ever have thought of me
Or planned for me
Or looked right through me
With future contemplation.
Right from the beginning of Time
I was all Your idea.
You had big things in mind for me
Good things, glorious things
And now, with magnificent dexterity
You are making them come to pass.
And I?
Well, I stand amazed on the sideline
And praise Your infinite patience.

THE MOUNTAIN

Dear Lord
I see it more clearly now:
Again and again I've begged You
To remove my mountain of difficulty—
While You have been patiently waiting
To cleanse my cluttered doubts
And calm my frantic fears
So I may climb the mountain.

INTIMACY

Dear God
May I live intimately close to You
Above the perplexities of Life
With the moon under my feet!
At the same time, God
Humble me, gentle me
Create in me a deepening awareness
So that I shall never miss
A cushion of violets hiding in the sod
Or the cry of a frightened child
Or the desperate sob of a lonely heart.

REFLECTION

Lord
Again and again I have asked You
To robe me in splendor—
To spark my life with radiance
Until there burns within me
A soft unquenchable glow.
Now today as I read Your Word
Your answer to my longing is so direct:
"They looked to him and were radiant."

Lord, the mystery is solved!
I must look steadfastly to You
For my radiance can only be
A shimmering reflection of Yours.

I CANNOT IMAGINE

God of my pensive heart
I cannot imagine
A day without the dawn
Or the sky without a star
Or a bird without a song
Or my life without You.

THIS BEAUTIFUL SUNLIT MORNING

Dear God
On this beautiful sunlit
Morning in May
You've drenched me
With ecstatic joy.
I want to sing and shout
I want to soar with sheer delight.
At the same time I want to sob—
So utterly overwhelmed I am
With the magnitude of You.

O God, I know
I do know
With serene satisfaction
And confident certainty
That I belong to the God
Of the Universe—
To the Creator
Of all that exists.

I do know
That I, a mere mortal
Am forever linked to divine destiny—
That my life has purpose and dignity.
I do know
That You have chosen me
As the object of Your lavish love
That Your thoughts toward me
Are thoughts of kindness and mercy
That You have inscribed me
In the palms of Your hands.

I do know
That all the Love of the Father
And the Life of the Son
And the Power of the Holy Spirit
Are freely, inseparably mine—
Now and through all eternity.
O God
On this beautiful sunlit
Morning in May
I do know.

I WONDER

The stars drift noiselessly
Over the silent sky
Like gently-kissed children
Drifting off to sleep.
I wonder, Lord—
Do You kiss the stars good-night?

YOU NAME THE STARS

God, I walked alone
In Your beautiful time
Called Night.
I lifted my face
To the soft-pillowed sky
And watched a shivering star
Fall out of bed—
And then I remembered:
That very star
You call by name!

THE TRUANT

Lord
What do You do with a truant
Who plays hooky from her Heavenly Parent?
What are the options?
One thing certain, You don't turn her off—
She's too noisy.
You don't pamper her because You know
She needs to stretch her spiritual muscles.
You don't shout, "Get up, foolish child"
Because she's covered with thick mud
From head to feet.
You don't condemn her because You said
"There is therefore now no condemnation . . . "

So in the end You do for her
What You always do for any bewildered

Half-demolished child of Yours:
You unlock her handcuffed spirit
With Your key of infinite love.
You check her fluctuating heart
With its spiritual irregularity.
When heart-to-heart resuscitation
Begins to revive her
You give her a fleeting glimpse
Of things as they could be.
Suddenly she knows with fresh gladness
That her one safe fortress
Is the center of Your will.
At least so it is with one truant . . .
Me.

PERMANENT HOOKUP

God
I am always getting one thing
Straightened out with You
And then another lion
Jumps out of the jungle.
Why couldn't You create
Some kind of permanent hookup
So life would stay
Settled, serene
And ecstatically spiritual!

Dear child
I have.
It's called Heaven.

CHRISTMAS IN JULY

In the middle of July
I found Christmas!
Jesus was born in the stall
Of my lonely heart.
He laid claim to every musty corner
Every dusty crevice
And from that day to this, O God
My heart has enthroned a King.

THERE IS EASTER!

Death seems so wrong, dear Lord
Couldn't You have remedied it?

Have you forgotten, dear child?
There is Easter!

RESURRECTION MORNING

O God
My life seems nothing more
Than an endless series
Of Good Fridays.
Please let me know
At least one
Resurrection morning.

First, dear child
You must die to yourself
And then you shall know
The unimaginable joy
Of walking out of the tomb.